AF593403

Sophy Chen World Poetry Translation Library (E-C Bilingual) 苏菲世界诗歌翻译书库（英汉对照）

A Poetry Collection of Dust by Qingdao Chen Yin
Translated by Sophy Chen
苏菲英译青岛尘音诗歌集《尘埃集》

尘埃集
Dust Poetry Collection

Language: Chinese and English Bilingual
语　言：汉英对照

Author: [China] Qingdao Chen Yin
作　者：[中国] 青岛尘音

Translator: [China] Sophy Chen / Lihua Chen
译　者：[中国] 苏　菲 ／ 陈丽华

Chief Editor: [China] Sophy Chen / Lihua Chen
主　编：[中国] 苏　菲 ／ 陈丽华
Assitant Editor: [China] Dazang Chen
副主编：[中国] 大 藏

苏菲国际翻译出版社
Sophy International Translation Publishing House

Sophy Chen's Some Words Before Translation And Publishing Of A Poetry Collection of Dust

—— Translation Foreword Of Sophy Chen

[China] Sophy Chen

In this colorful May full of wild flowers, Sophy International Translation Publishing House, Sophy International Publishing Media, Sophy Poetry & Translation (C-E) World Poetry Paper Magazine and Poetry Collections of Sophy Chen World Poetry Translation Library (Bilingual) welcome this exquisite Chinese poetry collection A Poetry Collection of Dust written by Qingdao Chen Yin from Qindao, China. In this romantic season of poetry writing, reading and translating, we can welcome this book which combines the poet's deep insight into the civilization of different times and his feelings of multiple life, society and natural philosophy....... is where the joy of life lies...

According to Qingdao Chen Yin, at first glance of his poet bio, it gives us a feeling of "both of he is in the present and not in the present". He, born in 1949, an engineer who studied science, began to write new poetry at the age of 20, in 1969. But to confuse to readers, he only started to publish his new poems online in 2011 and in 2017, his original Chinese poetry collection "A Poetry Collection of Dust" was published. His writing process, from 1969 to 2011, is in a full 42 years span. The poet has been writing, but has never published his works. To a poet, who has experienced a lot of patience and helplessness, many due to the reasons of the time and environment, the poet can only put his thoughts and feelings into writing, but not publicly published. Let us experience the ideal, pursuit and sadness of their generation and the life of the hope and helpless in his poems! Let's wait for this nice English and Chinese bilingual poetry collection giving birth !

苏菲写在《尘埃集》翻译出版前的几句话

——*苏菲翻译前言*

[中国] 苏　菲

在这个山花遍偏野、落英缤纷的五月，苏菲国际翻译出版社、苏菲国际出版传媒、《苏菲诗歌 & 翻译》（英汉世界纸质诗刊）社、《苏菲世界诗歌翻译书库》（汉英对照），迎来了这本由中国青岛诗人青岛尘音创作的精美现代诗歌集《尘埃集》。在这写诗、读诗、翻译诗的浪漫季节，能迎来这部融汇诗人对跨时代文明的深切洞察，对多重人生、社会、自然哲性感悟的著作，人生快意尽在其中……

青岛尘音，初看他的诗人简介，就给人一种“既入世而又出世”的感觉。生于 1949 年，一位学习理科的工程师，20 岁开始写新诗，那该是 1969 年开始写新诗。可是让读者不解的是，他 2011 年才开始在网络上发表新诗。2017 年出版汉语诗歌原创集“尘埃集”。他的写作历程，从 1969 年一直跨越到 2011 年，整整 42 年的时间跨度。诗人一直在创作，却从来没有公开发表过作品。这对于一位诗人，其中经历了多少隐忍与无奈，很多由于时代环境的原因，作者只能将所思所感诉诸笔端，却不便公开发表。就让我们从他的诗歌当中去体会，他们那一代对理想的追逐与心酸，对人生的期盼与无奈吧！就让我们静候这本精美的英汉双语诗歌集问世吧！

●序 篇

淘金者

青岛尘音

我们辛苦地淘洗着一座座的高山
我们付出的辛苦比高山更多、更多
只为得到那微少的闪光的报偿
但更多的时候，我们付出巨大的辛劳
却得不到丝毫的奖赏

我们的灵魂经常充满着卑俗的物质的欲望
心灵的幽暗的夜空没有一丝理想的星光
即使偶尔有灵感的闪电划破了阴暗的云层
但当笨拙的笔尖将它匆匆地记下
纸上的字句已失去了它原有的珍贵的灵光

2001.6.30

● Prologue

Gold Rush

Qingdao Chen Yin

We worked hard to wash the gold in high mountains by high mountains
We have worked for it more and even more than high mountains
Just to get the few flash of rewards
But most of time, we have paid a huge hard work
We can not get the slightest rewards

Our soul is often full of humble and material desires
There is no ideal starlight in the dark night sky of our soul
Even if there is an occasional inspiration lightning cutting through the dark clouds
When the clumsy pen tip record it in a hurry
The words on the paper have lost its original precious spiritual light

2001.6.30

CONTENTS 目 录

第二部分 咏 物
Section Two Praise of Objects

第三部分 沉 思
Section Three Meditation

第四部分 红 尘
Section Four Red Dust

世界诗歌评论 World Poetry Comments

作者后记 Author's Afterword

第一部分 尘 埃

Section One Dust

尘 埃

一缕阳光
照上我的书桌
无数尘埃
在阳光中闪烁浮动

我们生活着的星球
在茫茫宇宙中
是否也是这样地浮动着
并闪烁着蔚蓝色的光芒？

在这些闪烁的
浮动的尘埃上面
是否也生活着无数的
微小的可爱的生命

在那上面也曾上演过多少
他们自己的生活的戏剧
也曾有多少希望与失望
欢乐与悲伤？

1997．2．16

Dust

A beam of sunshine
Shines on my desk
The countless dust
Is flickering and floating in the sunlight

The planet which we live on
In the vast universe
Is floating like this or not
And shimmering with azure light?

Above these flickering
And floating dust
If there are also countless
Tiny, and lovely lives living

Above there how many dramas
Of their own lives have been played
How many hopes and disappointments
Joy and sorrow are there?

1997.2.16

吹糖稀的艺人

路边斜阳中，吹糖稀的艺人
用麦秆从锅中掘起一点糖稀
转瞬间就吹拉成一只可爱的动物
围观者们无不唏嘘赞叹

可是围观的人们
没人出钱去买他的作品
他只好叹口气将作品都投入锅中
挑起担子默默地走掉

在蓝色的天幕后面，造物者
在怎样地注视着我们
面对着他的作品，是满怀得意
还是充满了失望？

在我们难以预知的未来
当末日时刻来临的时候
他会将我们，连同我们的世界
都投入那巨大的锅中

2003.12

The Artist Blowing Golden Syrup To Candy

In the sun on the roadside, an artist who blows golden syrup to candy
Scooped a little golden syrup from the pot with wheat straw
And it was instantly blown into a cute animal
The onlookers were sighed and admired

But the onlookers
No one payed for his works
He had to sigh to throw his works into the pot
And took up his loaded carrying pole and walked away silently

Behind the blue sky, the Creator
How to look at us
Facing with his works, he was full of pride
Or full of disappointment?

In the future that we can't predict
When the doomsday comes
He will throw us, along with our world
Into that huge pot

2003.12

祈 祷

在这小小的星球上
有一群小小的我们
在这小小的天地之间
我们追求小小的幸福

在我们小小的生途之中
常常遇到小小的挫折
在我们小小的心灵里
常常充满着小小的痛苦

可是，当我们满怀小小的希望
常常得到小小的失望
当我们满含小小的失望
又常常得到小小的报偿

唉，虽然我们常犯些小小的过错
我们希望的只是一些可怜的小小
造物哟，请给这些小小的我们
以小小的恩赐，阿门！

1989．2．23

Prayer

On this little planet
There is a small group of us
Between this little sky and earth
We pursue our small happiness

In our little way of life
We often meet a small setback
In our little mind
It is often filled with a small pain

However, when we have a small hope
We often get a small disappointment
When we are full of small disappointment
We often get a small rewords

Alas, although we often make some small faults
What we want is just some little little poor
Creator, please give these little us
A little gift, Amen!

1989.2.23

帷 幕

我们曾经爱过、恨过
争取过、伤心过
但当希望实现时
却发现成功
并非想象那样美妙

我们曾经激昂过、愤怒过
奋斗过、悲恸过
但当理想实现时
却发现胜利
并非想象那样崇高

我们所追求的
不论多么美妙与崇高
但当那片帷幕落下
在造物者的面前
都是同样地卑微、渺小

1998

Curtain

We've loved and hated
Fought for, and had sadness
But when our hope has been achieved
We just discover that our success
Is not as wonderful as we've imagined

We've been excited and angry
Struggled, and sad
But when our ideal has been realized
We just find that our victory
Is not as high as we imagined

What we are pursuing
No matter how beautiful and lofty they are
But when the curtain has been fallen down
In front of the Creator
They are all humble, and small

1998

文 明

沙滩上的高塔
雄伟地耸立着
是雄心勃勃的男孩
精心建造的伟大作品

可是，每当他即将完成
空前伟大的事业
海浪总要恶作剧地嘻笑着
将高塔轻轻冲倒

1990．2．11

Civilization

The high tower on the beach
Majestic standing
Is a great works built carefully
By an ambitious boy

However, whenever he is about to complete
His unprecedented great cause
The waves have always gently swept down the tower
In laughing mischievously

1990.2.11

线

雄鱼搬运石子
为造幸福的窝

男人奔忙挣钱
为买豪华的住宅

傀儡在台上表演
艺人在后面拉线

造物者在世界的后面
手中拉着一根线

96．3．24

Thread

The male fish carries the stones
For making a happy nest

Men are busy to make money
For buying the luxury houses

Puppet performs on the stage
The actor pulls the thread behind

Creator is behind the world
There is a thread in his hands

96.3.24

禅

在苍生之上
在物欲之上
在痛苦之上
在执着之上

以深邃的微笑
以雍容的大度
以普照的慈光
照耀着我们

2011.8.10

Zen

Above the people
Above the material desire
Above the pain
On the persistance

With a deep smile
With gracious magnanimity
With the radiant and kind light
Shines on us

2011.8.10

晚霞中的后海

在繁华都市的边缘，偶尔一瞥晚霞中的后海
时间倾刻间凝固，喧嚣的市声也倏忽从耳畔消逝
辉煌的霞光笼罩着动荡的波光浩渺的海面
眩目的光涛荡漾在广阔无际的海天之间

光灿灿的金雕玉砌的仙山琼阁，令人惊心动魄地壮丽辉煌
色彩斑斓瑰丽的层峦叠嶂，闪烁着琳琅夺目的璀璨的魔光
使那最疯狂离奇、最奢华浩繁的想象也黯然失色
淋漓尽致地展示着造物者的雄奇奔放的伟大的创造力量

岸上熟悉的景物忽然变得陌生，平凡的世界忽然变得神秘
行人象是活动的金石雕塑，人们的神情更是那样庄重肃穆
寂静地林立的船桅象一片辽远神秘的高耸的塔楼
豪华幽深的高墙后面深藏着历尽沧桑的古老悲欢

深橙色的烟波中盘旋翻飞的群鸥象缤纷飞舞的炽热的火焰
整个世界都象在动荡沸腾的熔岩之海上浮动
巍峨的高楼之群忽然僵凝成一片猩红的惊愕的目光
错落的大树也停止摇动它们熊熊烈燃的火炬般的卷发

崇高而庄严的激情在大地和高天汹涌地激荡
灿烂的精神的光芒将世间的每一个角落照亮
从大地的深邃的心中喷涌出激越的澎湃的泪洪
绛红色的闪烁的大幕后面隐约传来悠远的亘古钟声

2001.9.26

Houhai In The Sunset

On the edge of the bustling city, when i occasionally catch a glimpse of the Houhai in the sunset
Time suddenly solidified, the noise of the city also disappeared from the ear
A brilliant glow enveloped the vast, turbulent sea
Blinding waves of light rippled across the vast expanse of sea and sky

The splendid golden and jade immortal mountains and castles are breathtaking in magnificence
The colorful and magnificent mountains, are flashing the dazzling bright magic light
It eclipses the wildest, strangest, most extravagant and voluminous imaginings
It vividly and incisively shows the great creative power of the creator

Familiar scene on shore suddenly becomes strange, ordinary world suddenly becomes mysterious
Pedestrians seem to be active in stone sculptures, their expressions are so solemn
The silent masts are like a mysterious tower in the distance
Behind these luxurious and deep walls lie the joys and sorrows of the past

The gulls whirled through the deep orange smoke like blazing flames in a riot of colors
The whole world seems to be floating on a turbulent and boiling sea of lava
The group of tall buildings suddenly froze into a scarlet stare of amazement
The scattered trees stopped shaking their torch-like curls

High and solemn passions were stirring on earth and in heaven
The light of the brilliant spirit illuminates every corner of the world
From the deep heart of the earth gushed a raging flood of tears
Behind the glowing crimson sky curtain came the faint sound of ancient bells

2001.9.26

蚂 蚁

我小时候，常常蹲在家门前
认真地观看蚂蚁的战争
那可不是两只蚂蚁打架
而是规模很大的战争

那场面非常激烈，
而且规模浩大
我似乎能听到
惊天动地的厮杀声

可是，母亲常常会大声喊着
快起来，闪开！
然后泼出一盆脏水
将战场冲得无影无踪

母亲肯定认为
蚂蚁的战争微不足道
但是蚂蚁们自己肯定认为
它们的战争与人类的战争同样地重要

2013.8

Ant

When I was young, I often squatted in front of my house
Watching the ants fighting seriously
That was not the fighting of two ants
But a large-scale war

That scene was very fierce
And in the vast scale
I seemed to be able to hear
The shattering sound of fighting

However, my mother often shouted loudly
Get up, get out of the way!
Then poured a pot of dirty water
To sweep the battlefield without a trace

My mother must think
Ant's war is insignificant
But the ants must think
Their war is as important as human war

2013.8

时 间

时间的坐标
并非沿直线前行
而是由许多
大小的圆弧构成

每转一圈
都会回到自己的原点
但又不完全是
原来的地方

我们存在于现在
但在每一瞬间
都仿佛能看到
祖先熟悉的面容

也许，在那个
命定的时刻
我们将会回到
时间的初始

2011.9.15

Time

The coordinates of time
Does not move along the straight line
Instead
Made by some small and big arcs

After it went a circle
It will return to its original point
But it is not exactly
Its original place

We exist at present
But at every moment
We seem to be able to see
The faces of our familiar ancestors

Maybe, in that
Destiny moment
We will return
The beginning of time

2011.9.15

蛙

井口是我们的苍天
井底是我们的大地
在这伟大的生命之井
我们歌唱生息

我们的视力有限
我们所处的井筒很深
可是我们的心比天高
以为我们能了解整个宇宙

假如有一天，宇宙的灼热的洪流
将我们抛出这小小的井筒
可是，这生命之井必定已遭毁坏
我们的生命之链也已灰飞烟灭

假如我们能逃过宇宙的灾变
侥幸到达那遥远的井口
可是我们怎能知道
我们距离真正的天穹还是很远，很远

2012.4.2

Frog

The mouth of sky is our sky
The bottom of the well is our land
In this great life well
We sing and live

Our vision is limited
The well in which we are is so deep
But our heart is higher than the sky
We think we can understand the entire universe

If one day, the hot torrent of the universe
Threw us out of this small well tube
However, the well of this life must be destroyed
The chain of our lives has also been disappeared

If we can escape the disaster of the universe
Fortunately, reach the distant well mouth
But how can we know
We are still far away from the real sky, far away

2012.4.2

云 帆

哦，那翻滚奔腾的洪流
隐现的闪烁的帆！
随波行进的航船哟
它从何而来，又要驶向何方？

哪里是它的源头？
哪里是它的归宿？
我们既不能测知这些
即使知道又有何用处！

它既不会有什么源头
也不会有任何海口
它只是沿着永恒的河床
不可抗拒地奔流

1975

Cloud Sails

Oh, the raging torrent
The looming twinkling sails!
A ship that travels with the waves
Where did it come from and where will it head for?

Where is it its source?
Where does it belong to ?
We can not measure any of this
It is useless even if you know what is!

It doesn't have a source
There won't be any seaport
It, just along the eternal riverbed
Flows irresistibly

1975

第二部分 咏 物

Section Two Praise of Objects

桃 核

春日的和风
明媚的阳光
欢畅与繁华
今在何方！

生活的风雨
世事的沧桑
已剥蚀尽
你的鲜艳与芬芳

高耸的向往
堕入时间的地层
鲜活的生命
已变得干枯僵硬

每一道深纹中
都记录着坎坷与彷徨
深锁的心中
仍有美丽的梦想

2000．2．6

Peach Pit

The soft breeze of spring
The bright sunshine
Happy and prosperous
Where is it today!

The wind and rain of life
Vicissitudes of the world
Have eroded
Your brightness and fragrance

Towering yearning
Fallen into the earth layer of time
Fresh life
Has become dry and stiff

In each deep pattern
It records both bumps and hesitation
In the heart of deep locks
There are still beautiful dreams

2000.2.6

琥 珀

滚烫的眼泪
是真情的见证
不论是快乐
或者苦痛

带有生命温度的泪水
落入时间的地层
就会凝结成珍贵的
闪光的结晶

把过往生活的点滴
发掘出时间的地层
都值得珍藏
可爱晶莹

2013.11.4

Chrysophoron

Hot tears
Is a testimony of true feelings
Regardless of happiness
Or painfulness

Tears with the temperature of life
Fall into the earth layer of time
It will condense into precious
And flashy crystal

To discover the little life in the past
Out of the stratum of time
Is worth of collecting
Cute and crystal

2013.11.4

高粱饴

质朴的端庄生于贫贱
爽滑的柔质出自粗涩
经历了漫长艰韧的磨练
造就了可爱高贵的资质

薄薄的铅华遮不住朦胧的晶莹
淡淡的甘甜回味更觉绵长
不必担忧浓烈甜蜜过后的辛酸
妖艳的华丽中有狠毒的尖刺潜藏

你的外表朴实无华
你的心怀温和善良
你的柔情回味无穷
你是温馨柔美的梦

2001．4．19

Sorghum Candy

Simplicity is born of poverty
Smooth softness comes from rough
After a long and difficult ordeal
It makes a lovely noble qualification

Thin lead can not cover the hazy crystal
Light sweet aftertaste is more lasting
Don't worry about the bitterness after the strong sweetness
In its coquettish splendor a vicious sting lurks

Your appearance is plain and simple
Your heart is gentle and kind
Your tender taste is endless
You are a sweet and soft dream

April 19, 2001

天 鹅

一片洁净的透明的云
一幅纯美的飘动的画
一曲舒缓的寂静的歌
一首空灵的无言的诗

在澄澈的晴空下
明镜般的湖面上
照耀着明丽的阳光
闪烁着华贵的光芒

生命的崇高的向往
美丽而宁静的理想
庄严之美的梦乡
心灵的圣洁的殿堂

2002．7．28

Swan

A piece of clean and transparent cloud
A beautiful and floating painting
A soothing and silent song
An ethereal and speechless poem

Under the clear and sunny sky
On the mirror-like lake surface
It shines the bright sunshine
And flashes the luxurious light

The lofty yearning of life
The beautiful and quiet ideal
The solemn dreamland
The holy hall of the soul

2002.7.28

猕猴桃

它的看相真不怎样
披头散发的流浪汉的形象
没精打采的看透一切的神情
随心所欲的不拘小节的做派

但一旦剥去那粗糙的外表
味道可是相当可口
而且营养极为丰富
是不修边幅的真正的艺术家

2013.11.21

Kiwi Fruit

He doesn’t look so good, does he
The image of a homeless man with disheveled hair
The slouchy look of knowing everything
A freewheeling, informal style

But once you strip away his rough exterior
He tastes quite delicious
He is extremely nutritious
He is a true artist of unkempt

2013.11.21

坛 子

在博物馆的
恒温恒湿的玻璃罩里
一只古代普通的坛子
是无价之宝

在贫穷的农舍里
同样的坛子
只是用来
盛装食盐

两只坛子的价值
有什么不同
它们的价值
与时间有关

食盐是生命的必需
但它很廉价
时间虽然无色无味
但它是无价的

2011.9.15

Jar

In a museum-based glass case
With constant temperature and humidity
An ancient common jar
Is priceless

In a poor farmhouse
The same jar
Just for
Putting salt

The value of two jars
What's the difference
Their value
Is dependent on time

Salt is essential to life
But it's cheap
Time is colorless and tasteless
But it's priceless

2011.9.15

隼

浩荡的劲风和热烈的阳光
在高空交织着光与力的巨网
浩瀚的奔放的松林和海洋
苍穹下充满着它们的气息和喧响

云中的王者，在翻腾的云团之上翱翔
钢羽搅动劲风，镶满炽红的阳光
时而如黑色的闪电掠过动荡的松涛和海浪
时而如腾空的利箭直插苍茫

自由地翻飞，傲岸地高翔
高洁的心灵在高空豪迈地歌唱
与松涛与海浪汇成恢弘的乐章
在环宇之间雄浑地轰响

2001．3．21

Hawk

The mighty strong wind and the warm sunshine
Are interweaving the giant network of light and force over the high sky
The vast and unrestrained pine forest and ocean
Are full of their breath and noise under the sky

The king in the clouds is soaring on the rolling cloud clusters
His steel feathers, inlaid with red sunlight, are stirring up the strong wind
Sometimes like a black lightning passing through the turbulent pine trees winds and waves
Sometimes like a flying sharp arrow striking straight into the vastness

Flying freely, soaring proudly
His noble-minded heart sings proudly in high sky
Combining into the magnificent movement with pine trees winds and waves
And making a big noise between the universes

2001.3.21

蛾

远方的光明
指引着风雨兼程
辉煌的希望之光
将心灵照亮

险恶的艰难
不能改变坚定的信念
惊心动魄的风暴雷霆
不能阻挡奋勇向前

当理想终于实现
忽然眼前一片黑暗
一阵彻骨的疼痛
周身化为焦烟

灵魂飞舞着
燃烧的火焰
悲壮地献身在
理想的祭坛

2001．2．27

Moth

The light of the distance
Guides the way in wind and rain
The glory hope light
Illuminates the mind

The sinister difficulty
Can’t change firm beliefs
The thrilling storm and thunder
Can’t stop forge ahead

When the ideal is finally realized
Suddenly the darkness in front of his eyes
A pain in his bone
His whole body turns into a smoke burnt

One with his soul flying
In the burning flame
Silently dedicated to
IIis idcal altar

2001.2.27

桃

它有鲜艳的色彩
虽说有点暧昧
但没有刺眼的反光
有某种柔和的美

它的味道比较酸甜平和
是人们喜欢的口味
而且内外比较一致
不像有的果子越往深处越酸

就算它贡献了自己的一生
只剩下一颗坚硬的内核
最后还是准备奉献
它的芬芳的内心

2013.11.19

Peach

It has bright colors
It is a little vague
Though there's no glare light
There's a certain soft beauty

Its taste is more sweet and sour
It's a taste that people like
And it is consistent inside and out
It's not like some fruits get sour as going to deeper of it

Even if it gave its life
Only a hard core was left
Finally, it prepares to give
Its fragrant heart

2013.11.19

苹 果

第一个苹果
被亚当夏娃吃掉
创造了人类

第二个苹果
砸在牛顿的头上
创造了工业时代

第三个苹果
被乔布斯咬了一口
创造了一个硅谷奇迹

祈望我们的苹果
及时落下
在它没烂掉之前

2011,9.4

Apple

The first apple
Eaten by Adam and Eve
Created man

Second apple
It fell on Newton's head
Created the industrial age

The third apple
Got bitten by Jobs
Created a miracle of Silicon Valley

Pray for our apples
Fall in time
Before it rots

2011,9.4

昙 花

微微颤抖着
承受着夜露的滋养
展现着纯洁的恐惧与渴望
在寂静的风暴中摇曳

在长久的沉默和等待之后
在无数的朦胧的梦幻之后
终于在一个意想不到的瞬间
轰响生命最美的乐章

2015.1.14

Epiphyllum

It shivers slightly
Nourished by the night dew
Showing pure fear and desire
Swaying in the storm of silence

After a long silence and waiting
After countless hazy dreams
Finally in an unexpected moment
It booms the most beautiful music of life

2015.1.14

蜜三刀

任何甜蜜
都难逃收税的刀

第一刀还算温柔
减轻恐怖的痛

第二刀有点严重
毁坏珍贵的面容

第三刀最残忍
刺在心头

2011.10.10

Three Honey Knives

Any sweet
It can not escape the knife of tax

The first cut was gentle
To relieve the pain of terror

The second cut is a little serious
To destroy precious faces

The third cut is the most cruelest
To stab in the heart

2011.10.10

喇叭花

在僻静的小路
旁边的山岩上
有一朵蓝色的喇叭花
在静静地开放

象一颗寂寞的小星星
在清冷的微风中轻轻摇晃
它略带羞怯的目光中
似乎流露着淡淡的忧伤

2011.9.20

Trumpet Flower

On a quiet road
Next to the rocks
There is a blue trumpet flower
Blossoming in silence

Like a lonely little star
Swaying gently in the cool breeze
It's slightly sheepish in the eyes
There seems to be a hint of sadness

2011.9.20

蝉

蝉的种族
大约有两类
一类叫诗人
一类叫哲学家

激动的诗人
热情地高歌：啊!
深沉的哲学家
郑重地宣布：知啦!

他们是生灵界中
最清高的动物
在那崇高的枝头
只需餐风饮露

1998．8．4．

Cicada

Cicada race
There are about two categories
One is called poet
Another is called philosopher

The excited poet
Sings with enthusiasm: Ah!
The deep philosopher
Solemnly declares: I know!

Among the creatures they are
The most noble animal
In the lofty branches
They just eat the wind and drink the dew

1998.8.4.

猫屎咖啡

乍听真是吃惊不小
再听还真是那么回事
我真是服了
人啊，怎么会这样!

都说人类的进化
是向着美的方向挺进
人们为什么前进几步
就会留恋地回望?

2011.8.17

Cat Poop Coffee

What a surprise to hear
Well, that sounds like a real story
I'm really impressed
People, how can this happen!

They say human's evolution
Is moving in the direction of beauty
Why do people take steps forward
They will look back nostalgically?

2011.8.17

圆 葱

在聚光灯的交射中
表情凝重的魔术师
将魔布一层层掀开
音乐洪水般汹涌

在庄严的期待之后
在热泪盈眶之中
辛辣的玩笑
意外的结局

2011.9.27

Onion

Cross light fire in the spotlight
A magician with a serious expression
Is lifting the cloth a layer by a layer at a time
In a flood of music

After solemn anticipation
With tears in my eyes
In a biting joke
There is an unexpected ending

2011.9.27

第三部分 沉 思

Section Three Meditation

沉 思

哦，昔日那美丽的金色的彩虹
少年时代的纯洁的憧憬
珍贵的时光老人的赠品呀
别了，天真而灿烂的幻梦！

风啊，吹散了花冠
它也不会重生
生活只留下愧恨的记忆
和创伤的余痛

Meditation

Oh, the beautiful and golden rainbow in the past
The pure dream of the young age
The precious time, the gift for the elderly
Farewell, the naive and brilliant fantasy!

Wind oh, blown away the corolla
It will not be reborn
Life only left the ashamed memory
And the traumatic pain

风 景

有一次，我沿着一条小路前行
在一处美景前流连忘返
直到傍晚才返回
可是后来发现
在小路的前面有更美的风景

后来，我沿着另一条小路前行
走过了几处挺美的风景
总想遇到更美的风景
可是直到傍晚，走到了小路的尽头
也没遇到更美的风景

2014.7.3

Scenery

Once, I walked along a path
Forgot to return before a beautiful scenery
And returned until the evening
But later I discovered
There was a more beautiful scenery in front of the path

Later, I walked along another path
After I walked along a few beautiful scenery
I always wanted to meet a more beautiful scenery
But until the evening, to the end of the path
I did not encounter a more beautiful scenery

2014.7.3

珍 惜

我们站在大河岸边
感慨地凝望涌动的旋流滚滚向前
在不知不觉中，河水已流蚀过我们的脚下
蓦然发现自己已在河中漂流

我们埋头读着先人的历史
脑海中激荡着祖先们的忧乐、业绩
在不知不觉中，流光染白了我们的鬓发
蓦然发现自己已被陌生的后人阅读

可是，当沉思的灵猿
不再为镜中陌生的自己而好奇
明亮的镜面已被时间的流沙磨蚀
他们已经不能重新发现自己

1989．2．25

Cherish

We, standing on the bank of the big river
Are looking at the rolling water surging forward in high emotion
Unconsciously, the river has eroded under our feet
Suddenly I found that I had drifted in the river

We are seriously reading the history of the ancestors
In our mind, the ancestors' worry and performance
Unconsciously, the streamer bleached our hair at the temples
Suddenly I found that I have been read by my unfamiliar posterity

However, when the spiritual apes
Are no longer curious about the strange self in the mirror
The bright mirror has been eroded by the sands of time
They can no longer discover themselves

1989.2.25

轮 回

物质的花朵在光明中
才能展示它的绚烂的色彩
精神的火炬在黑暗中
才能彰显它的崇高与辉煌

在黑暗中
我们追求光明与温暖的阳光
在光明中
我们又怀念庄严崇高的殿堂

在纯粹的光明中
就像
在纯粹的黑暗中
都会使我们迷失方向

2013.12.20

Reincarnation

The material flower in the light
Can show its gorgeous colors
The torch of the spirit in the darkness
Can show its lofty and glory

In the darkness
We pursue lights and warm sun
In the light
We miss the solemn and lofty hall

In the pure light
Just like
In the pure darkness
All of them will make us lose our direction

2013.12.20

可 能

过分猛烈的笑
可能使人流泪

过度强烈的光线
可能使眼睛失明

奇特地艳丽的花
可能有狠毒的刺

离奇地美好的境界
可能是魔鬼的布施

1981．2．

Probablity

Laughing too hard
May bring tears

Excessive intensity of light
May cause blindness in the eyes

Strangely showy flowers
Could have a venomous sting

The realm of uncanny beauty
Could be a gift from the devil

1981.2.

实 现

我喜爱鲜花
但被它狠毒地刺痛

我向往大海
但几乎在那里丧生

我珍视友情
但被卑鄙地出卖

我追求光明
但到近前要戴上墨镜

1981.4

Realize

I love flowers
But stung viciously

I yearn for the sea
But almost died there

I value friendship
But betrayed despicably

I seek the light
But have to wear sunglasses before got closed of it

1981.4

不 幸

任何幸福都应缴纳重税
在我们生命的途中
幸福与痛苦
总是相伴同行

不受痛苦的幸福
是卑鄙
不为幸福的痛苦
是愚昧

然而不幸的是
在我们的身边
太多愚昧的卑鄙
又太少伟大的愚昧

1998．7．9

Unhappiness

Any happiness should pay heavy taxes
On the way to our lives
Happiness and pain
Always walk with each other

The happiness without suffering
Is despicable
The pain not for happiness
Is ignorant

But unfortunately
By our side
Too much ignorant meanness
Too little great ignorance

1998.7.9

呐 喊

在生命的桥头
我们呐喊
伴随着血腥和巨痛
我们跨越生死

在历史的桥头
我们呐喊
伴随着血腥和巨痛
我们跨越时代

2008.1.11

Shout

On the bridge head of life
We shout
Accompanied by blood and great pain
We've crossed life and death

In the bridge head of history
We shout
Accompanied by blood and great pain
We've crossed the times

2008.1.11

高仓健

从水深火热的
漫长的中世纪的
毒焰沸腾的最后的暗夜
刚刚走出的中国人

恍如隔世般惊诧地见到
具有人的尊严的
陌生的，冷峻深沉的表情
心灵的震动难以表述

在那以前的年代
我们见得太多的是
从太监式的极尽卑鄙无耻的山呼万岁的狂热的冰糖脸
瞬间变幻为凶狠残暴的恶魔面孔

高仓健，象一阵清新的风
吹散了腐朽恶浊的中世纪的气息
和那太不拿自己当人的
可悲的恐怖的中国式的变脸术

2014.11.19

Takakura Ken

Chinese just come out
From the last night of the poisonous flame boiling
The long middle ages
The deep water and burning fire

When they see surprisingly as if being cut off from the outside world for ages
The unfamiliar, cold and deep expression
In human dignity
The vibration of their soul is difficult to express

In that time before
What we see too much
Are the fierce and brutal demon faces instantly changed
From eunuch-style, shameless sugar faces, loudly calling their monarch long live as mountains

Takakura Ken, like a fresh wind
Blows the breath of the decaying and turbid medieval century
And the sad and horrible Chinese-style face-changing
That doesn't take himself as a human too much

2014.11.19

钢 笔

若在那阳光灿烂的窗前
在春风醉人的吹拂之中
我提起了闪光的钢笔
心中有万千支号角怒鸣

当流星划过严寒的夜空
蓝色的闪光曳出紫黑色的喷迸
那是正义与信念
在行施神圣的使命

当我的激动的笔锋
搅扰了稿纸的平静
那里将滚动着钢铁的铿锵
和雷电的轰隆

当我的短剑在风暴中嘶吼
这钢铁的笔锋
将去刻写壮烈的诗章
剖开猩红的黎明

1974

The Pen

If in front of the sunny window
In intoxicating blowing of the spring breeze
I held a shinning pen
There are thousands of horns calling angrily in my heart

When the meteor passes through the frosty cold night sky
The blue flash pulls out the purple and black spray
That is the justice and belief
Surging in sacred mission

When my excited pen
Breaks the calm of the manuscript paper
There will be rolling the ring voice of steel
And the bombardment voice of light and thunder

When my short sword growls in the storm
The tip of steel pen
Will write the magnificent poems
And split the scarlet dawn

1974

红

高级生命的
内在的颜色
一旦暴露
就是恐怖与死亡

最美的怒放的
花朵的颜色
看得太多
却会伤害视力

我们梦寐以求的
永恒的憧憬
至真至美的
文明进步的花朵

为什么喜欢
那么多的生命
和那么多的
滚烫的热血

2013.11.5

Red

The inner color
Of the advanced life
Once exposed
It is terror and death

The color of flowers
The most beautiful and blooming
But to be seen too much
It can hurt the vision of us

The eternal vision
Dreamed by us
The civilized and progressive flowers
True and beautiful

Why they like
So many life
And so much
Hot blood

2013.11.5

荒 沙

人最大的痛苦
是没有什么值得去死
而活着又不知为了什么

被海市蜃楼愚弄得太久
一旦看清使他激动的一切
心田也将被荒沙淹没

1991．3．1

Deserted Sand

What the greatest pain to a man
Is that nothing is worth going to die
And he does not know what to do on life

It was too long to be fooled by the mirage
Once he sees clearly everything that makes him excited
His mind will be overwhelmed by the deserted sand

1991.3.1

梦

我曾梦见
我从梦中的
梦中觉醒

我一次又一次地
从睡床上坐起来
艰难地睁开眼睛

但每一次的觉醒
都只是在下一次觉醒的
梦中

我蓦然心惊：
难道此时此刻
我仍然还在梦中？！

1988．8．21

Dream

I dreamed that
I got awaken from a dream that
Is from another dream

I do it again and again
Sit up from bed
Struggling to open my eyes

But in every awakening
I am all just waking up the dream's awaken
Of the next time

I was suddenly shocked:
Is this the moment
I am still dreaming? !

21 August 1988

古铜色的梦

象陌生世界的
信息的遥感
又象前世印象的
遥远的梦幻

古铜色的天上
浮着古铜色的云团
古铜色的天光
照耀着古铜色的河面

古铜色的曲折的
古老的岩岸
披满古铜色的
潮湿的苔藓

古铜色的石砌的
巍峨的宫殿
古铜色的闪烁的
高耸的塔尖

古铜色皮肤的
沉静的少年
轻轻摇着那
古铜色的小船

别了，那黯然逝去的
忧伤的童年
和那难忘时光的
遥远的梦幻

1984．5．13

The Bronzed Dream

It is like in a strange world
The remote sensing of information
It is also like the distant dream
Of the impression of a previous life

In the bronze sky
There were clouds of bronze
The bronze sky light
Is shining on the bronzed river

The old rocky shore
Of the distant dream
Draps the bronzed colour
Damp moss

A magnificent palace
Of bronze colour stones
The towering spire
Of Shimmering bronze

With a tan
And quiet teenager
Shaking gently
A tan boat

Farewell, all sadness gone
Sad childhood
And that distant dream
Of unforgettable time

May 13, 1984

花坛秋暮

啊，往日的美丽的花冠早已凋零
也褪尽了闪烁的眩目的金红
显赫的朝露变成了秋暮的霜棱
心儿也空寂了无谓的论争

别了，那如云霞飞逝的飘渺的韶光
绛紫色的沉醉荡魄的馨风
那如浮光流转的变幻的青春
花团锦簇的深沉的迷梦

1981．10．25

The Flower Bed In The Late Autumn

Ah, the beautiful crown of the past has long gone
And faded its blinding gold and red color
The illustrious morning dew has changed into the frost edges of autumn twilight
My heart is empty of useless arguments

Farewell, the misty time that flies like rose clouds
Purplish intoxicating spirit of the wind
The changing youth as floating light circulation
And deep dreams of flowers

October 25, 1981

瞬 间

一缕阳光照上我的憔悴的脸
眼前立刻现出一片五彩的花团
我永不会忘记那美妙的时刻
那神思飞扬的光辉的瞬间

1981．10．25

Instance

A ray of sunshine shines on my haggard face
In front of my eyes a colorful flower immediately appeared
I will never forget that wonderful moment
The glorious moment of the mind

October 25, 1981

桃花扇

本该在香艳的风中
摇曳生姿
但却在恐怖豪华的故事里
讲述儒生商女的绝代柔情

在历史的桥头
西风残照
宏伟的古老的宫殿与帝陵
血色的黄昏与黎明

2015.7.17

The Peach Blossom Fan

You should have been in the fragrant wind
Swaying your posture
But in a horror and luxury story
Tell the unmatched tenderness of Confucian and businessman woman

At the bridge of history
The west wind is shining
On the magnificent old palaces and imperial tombs
The bloody dusk and dawn

2015.7.17

椭 圆

人们一般认为圆最完美
但椭圆比圆更完美
比如：桌子、镜子、脸和眼睛
有广告说：没有最好，只有更好

在和谐与狂暴之间
在天堂与地狱之间
事物关系的完美逻辑
我们深心真善美的真谛

是自然的和谐的、不是人为的拙劣的
是运动的进取的、不是停滞的腐朽的
是智慧的光明的、不是愚昧的黑暗的
是平等的尊严的、不是强暴的奴性的

我们生存于椭圆的世界
沿着椭圆的轨迹运行
让我们赞美，让我们遵循
伟大的、永恒的椭圆

1993．11．11

Ellipse

Circles are generally considered the most perfect
But an ellipse is more perfect than a circle
For example: table, mirror, face and eyes
There is an advertisement that says: there is no best, but only better

Between harmony and fury
Between heaven and hell
The perfect logic of the relationship of things
The true meaning of truth, goodness and beauty we are deeply committed to

Is the natural harmony, not man-made ineptness
Is the progressive movement, not the stagnant decay
Is the light of wisdom, not the darkness of ignorance
Is the equal dignity, not violent servility

We live in an elliptical world
Follow an elliptical trajectory to go
Let us praise, let us follow
The great, eternal ellipse

1993.11.11

远方的云

人们在家乡时
会向往远方的云
人们远在异乡时
又会向往故乡的云

人们往往将眼光
投向远方
却往往忽略了
当下的风景

2013.9.22

Distant Clouds

When people are in their hometown
We will yearn for the distant clouds
When people are far away from home
We will yearn for the clouds of our hometown

People tend to look
Into the distance
But often ignore
Current landscape

2013.9.22

战争与女人

战争让女人离开
并非说二者无关
实际上恰恰相反

古希腊的那场著名的战争
千万的将士葬身沙场
据说将士们都认为死有所值

狮王用尿液划定疆界
它的王国
就是它的后宫

爱情与幸福都难免竞争
让我们告别尿液与爪牙
进化为文明的君子之争

2011.12.30

War And Women

War makes women go away
And they say they are unrelated with war
In fact, it is quite the opposite

The famous war in ancient Greece
Tens of thousands of soldiers died on the battlefield
It is said that soldiers think death is worth of it

The lion sets the boundaries with his urine
Its kingdom
Is its harem

Love and happiness are both in competition
Let's say goodbye to urine and pawns
Evolve into a civilized gentleman's struggle

2011.12.30

冰 花

在严寒的冬天
窗玻璃的画板上
精心描绘出
奇异的画面

巨大的叶片
粗大的枝干
幽暗的丛林
奇异的植被

那是严冬心中
对繁荣时光
深沉的向往
最瑰丽的梦！！

2011.9.27

Ice Flowers

In the cold winter
On the drawing board of window glass
The strange pictures
Are carefully depicted

The huge leaves
The rough branches
The dark jungle
The strange vegetation

That is in the heart of cold winter
The best time
The deep longing
The most magnificent dream!!

2011.9.27

第四部分 红 尘

Section Four Red Dust

命 运

每当新的一天来临
面对一片灿烂的霞光
都会触发我们的壮丽的遐想
心中充满无限的欢畅
和对未来生活的美好的希望

每当新的时代来临
面对一片辉煌的希望之光
我们都会欢呼雀跃、热泪盈眶
真诚地相信我们世代憧憬的千年盛世已经来临
即将实现我们永恒的梦想

就这样，我们心中满怀着对未来生活的美好的希望与梦想
走过生途中无数惊心动魄的艰难险阻和坎坷彷徨
一天又一天，一代又一代
在生活的舞台上创造着人生的悲喜交集的戏剧
在命运之路上走过生命的希望与奋争、辉煌与悲壮

2000.6.20

Destiny

Whenever a new day comes
Facing a brilliant glory
It will trigger our magnificent reveries
Our heart will be full of unlimited joy
And the beautiful hope for future life

Whenever a new era comes
Facing a glorious light of hope
We will cheer, in hot tears
We'll sincerely believe that the thousand-year-old prosperous age of our generation has arrived
It's about to realize our eternal dream

In this way, our hearts are full of hope and dreams of good future life
There are countless thrilling difficult and dangerous obstacles and bumps on the way of our life
Day after day, generation after generation
We create the drama in happy and tragic intersection of life on the stage of life
We walk on the road of life in hope and struggle, glory and tragedy of life

2000.6.20

花 季

晴天的小雨
激情的眼泪
晶莹的泪珠
挂满花蕾

晴天的白云
透明的微笑
晶莹的花蕾
含笑微微

晴天的微风
柔情的发丝
悄悄的微笑
红透的花蕾

有风才有云
有云才有雨
有情才有爱
世界才美丽

1997．2．13

Flowering Season

The light rain in sunny days
Tears of passion
Crystal tears
Hangs on buds of flowers

White clouds in sunny days
Transparent smile
Crystal flower buds
Laughs a little

Breeze in sunny days
Tender hair
Quiet smile
Is the red flower buds

There is a wind, there is a cloud
There is a cloud, there is a rain
There is a feeling, there is a love
The world will be beautiful

1997.2.13

傻 笑

高山顶上的草
会长得矮小
生命高峰上的人
只会含泪傻笑

在日常生活中
人们斗志昂扬
一旦动了真情
立刻缴械投降

犀利机警的目光
会变得泪眼迷离
冷若冰霜的高傲
会变得温和谦虚

在上帝的面前
没有什么尊卑
在真情的面前
没有什么美丑

1998．8．2

Giggle

Grass on the top of the mountain
Will grow short
People at the peak of life
Can only giggle with tears

In daily life
People fight in high spirit
Once we are moved by our true feelings
We immediately do surrender

The sharp and alert eyes
Will become tearful and blurred
The pride as ice and frost
Will become gentle and humble

In the presence of God
There is no honorable and humble
In the face of true feelings
There is no beauty and ugly

1998.8.2

红 尘

华贵的金碧辉煌
雄浑的生命的交响
在灿烂的阳光中
苍蝇之群飞舞

金光闪烁的门扉喷薄着雄辩
播种着恐怖与死亡
黑色的惊雷掠过灰色的天幕
在庄严的雕栏玉砌之上

肥沃的金马之泉
养育着伟大的生命链
黄褐色的浓稠的汁液中
洁白的肉体劲舞狂欢

明灭缤纷的旋光中
惊心动魄的幽灵疯狂地痉挛
污水般奔涌的音响里
聒噪着怪兽的吼喊

1995．7．10

Human Society

The luxurious and resplendent
Vigorous symphony of life
A swarm of flies was flying
In the bright sunshine

The golden doors glows with eloquence
Sowing terror and death
Black thunder swept over the gray sky
On a stately fence of jade

The fertile spring of golden horses
Nurtures the great chain of life
In yellowish brown and thick juice
White flesh are dancing in carnival

In the colorful swirling light
The thrilling apparition convulsed wildly
In a sound system that gushes like sewage
Is noisy with the roar of the monster

1995.7.10

拟 古

秋又至，落叶纷旋，朔风初肃
怅秋风，荡涤尘沙，画角迟暮
休再去痴心执着鼓与呼
望天高云巧，收拾烦绪，归我敝庐

莫再妄议是与非，虽谓吾侪皆凡俗
人心向来深难测，更那堪愚鲁难免为人误
偷闲而已，岂愚顽妄意荣与辱
自此后，悉心孔方，留心俗务，自斟粗茶
重隐江湖

2013.10.6

Model Oneself After the Ancients

Autumn is coming again, falling leaves are swirling and north wind are flowing early
Melancholy autumn wind, washes the dust and sand and late painting corner
Just stop to infatuate the persistent drum and shout
Look up to the sky, clean up the trouble, and go back to my cottage

Don't talk about right and wrong, though we are common
The heart has always been difficult to measure, but it is hard to avoid being mistaken
It is only idle time, no fool wants honor or disgrace
From then on, just took care of my own customs, and make my own tea
And disappear again in the rivers and lakes

2013.10.6

留 守

父母远在他乡
孩子留守在家
在破旧的土屋前
在炫目的阳光下
思念中的孩子沉默不语

在记者借用的手机前
孩子的泪象决堤的水
就是铁石心肠也会心碎
我们这些没出息的大人
真该为自己的失落惭愧

他们家中没有大人
小小年纪就自己做饭
唯一的菜是一碟盐
在贫瘠的土路上
寂寞的孩子牵着毛驴前行
沉默的背影让人心痛

2011.8.20

Stay Behind For Garrison Duty

Parents are far away
Children stay at home
In front of the old mud hut
In the blinding sun
The missing child is silent

In front of a phone borrowed by a reporter
The tears of the child are like water breaking the bank
Even a heart of stone can have its heart broken
We grown-ups who are unuseful
I should be ashamed of my loss

They have no adults at home
Cooking for themselves at a young age
The only dish is a dish of salt
On a barren dirt road
The lonely child leads the donkey
The silent back hurts me

2011.8.20

好 人

久已从我们语言中消失的词汇
乍听还真有点不太习惯
被冰河世纪冷透的身心
要缓解过来真还需要时间

习惯了大鄙灭亲的严重黑脸
要忽然扮作一张慈祥的笑颜
已经长久僵硬的面部肌肉
要想迅速松弛还不太习惯

2011.9.5

Good Person

Words that have long disappeared from our language
I'm not used to it at first
The body and mind chilled by the ice age
It's going to take time to get over this

I'm used to the bad, dirty face of the family
If suddenly i need to put on a kind smile
Facial muscles that have been stiff for a long time
I'm not used to relaxing quickly

2011.9.5

思 绪

我努力整理一团乱麻
可总是不能弄整齐
最后只好揉成一团扔掉

我努力整理纷乱的思绪
可总是不能弄清楚
最后还是将它们珍藏在深心

1991．3．20

Thought

I tried to sort out the mess
But I can't get it straight
Finally i had to crumple it up and throw it away

I tried to organize my confused thoughts
But i always can not figure it out
In the end, I kept them in my deep heart

1991.3.20

孤 影

残冬的懒散的阳光
透过清晨迷离的烟雾
把我的朦胧的孤影
投向前面沉默的道路

1984．3．31

Lone Shadow

The lazy sunshine of late winter
Through the misty haze of the morning
Throws my hazy lonely shadow
To the silent road ahead

1984. 3. 31

臭豆腐

我不反对
人们对食物
品味的多样化
不过，有些喜好
可以作为点缀
不宜成为主流

2011.8.17

Fermented Bean Curd

I have no objection of
Diversity of taste of
People's attitude towards food
But some preferences
May serve as embellishment
Out of the mainstream

2011.8.17

关于臭豆腐

我有时
也想尝试
但始终
不敢

就怕
一旦尝试
会养成某种
坏习惯

2011.8.18

About Fermented Bean Curd

Sometimes I...
Also want to try
But always
Dare not

Be afraid of
Once tried
I will develop a certain
Bad habit

2011.8.18

曼德拉

平等与自由的斗士
宽容与和解的旗帜
他是人类的骄傲
他是空前的英雄

他的胸怀象大海
象高天那样广阔
他的宽容的笑容
是人类永恒的良知

2013.12.6

Mandela

A fighter for equality and freedom
A banner of tolerance and reconciliation
He is the pride of mankind
He is an all-time hero

His bosom is like the sea
As wide as the heavens
His forgiving smile
Is the eternal conscience of mankind

2013.12.6

游 子

从前，我常常趁母亲去晾衣裳
把纸船放进洗衣盆
让它载着我幼稚的理想
在幻想的大海上乘风破浪

可是，忙碌的母亲
总是把水与船一起泼光
粗心的母亲哟
你可知道孩子的忧伤？

今天，我远离久已隔绝的母亲
常常乘船航行在遥远的海洋
我领略过令人目眩的奢华和奔忙
惊叹过那些稀世的山色湖光

可是，不管我在世界上什么地方
我的心总是留在母亲身旁
我久违的故乡、母亲哟
你可知道游子的惆怅？

1984．6

Traveler

In the past, when my mother went to dry clothes
I often put the paper boat in the laundry basin
And let it carry my naive ideals
Going in the wind on the sea of fantasy

However, my busy mother
Always poured the water with the boat together
My careless mother, oh
Do you know the sadness of your child?

Today, I've stayed away from my mother isolated for a long time
I often sail by boat in the distant ocean
I've appreciated the dazzling luxury and hustle
I've been amazed by those rare mountains and lakes

But no matter where I am in the world
My heart always stays beside my mother
My hometown and mother that I've been away for a long time, oh
Do you know the melancholy of a traveler?

1984.6

窥 视

眼睛！眼睛？
猥琐而冷酷
愚昧而凶残
灰绿色的寒光

从每个卑鄙、狡诈的洞孔
从每个肮脏阴暗的角落
从每道意想不到的缝隙中
战栗地、惊心动魄地窥视

恶心的风暴
掠过悲凉的天穹
悲恸的世界
在血泪中漂流

2001．2．10

Spy On

Eyes! Eyes?
Wretched and cold
Ignorant and cruel
A cold gray-green light

From every mean, and cunning hole
From every dirty, and dark corner
From every unexpected crevice
A thrilling and shuddering spying

The nasty storm
Across the sad dome of heaven
A world of mourning
Is drifting in blood and tears

2001.2.10

散步有感

道路尽头升起的太阳
把我面前的道路照亮
任凭那阴影追随着我
怎能把我的前程阻挡

1984．5．20

Walking Feel Good

The sun rising at the end of the road
Gives the path light before me
Let the shadow follow me
How can it stand in the way of my future

1984.5.20

遗 嘱

母亲在年老后
曾多次平静地
用浓重的乡音
对我这样叮嘱

等我死了
抬出去就行
不用破费
什么也不用

是的，人生总有诀别的时刻
这是生命永恒的悲剧
但我每当听到这里
总是转过脸，泪下如雨

2011.7

Testament

Mother in old age
Many times calmly
In a strong local accent
Tells me so

When I die
Just carry me out
At no cost
Don't need anything

Yes, there are moments in life when we say goodbye
This is the eternal tragedy of life
But every time I hear this
I always turn my face,with tears raining down

2011.7

早晨的印象

伴随着群鸟的合唱
第一缕初春的明媚的阳光
光明与温暖的洪流
注满了我粉白的卧房

当我还在迷离的悠远的
梦的世界的边缘彷徨
而新春的欢快的气息
就沸腾着涌进了我的心房

在狂喜的战栗中激跳的心里
展现着壮阔的辉煌的影像
这也许就是我许久以来的热烈的憧憬
对人类未来的最纯美的期望

1980．3

Morning Impression

With the chorus of birds
The first bright sunshine of early spring
The flood of light and warmth
Fill my pink and white bedroom

When I'm still wandering on the edge of the dream world
In the twilight of the distant
And the happy breath of the New Year
Is boiling into my heart

In a shudder of ecstasy a heart beating
Shows images of magnificent splendor
This may be my long and warm longing
The purest hope for the future of mankind

1980.3

足 迹

海滩上静悄悄
没有人群和欢笑
在晚秋的寒风中
夕阳斑斓的光华
把人们的足迹照耀

1981.

Foot Marks

The beach was quiet
No crowds and laughter
In the cold wind of late autumn
The gorgeous glow of the setting sun
Shine people's footprints

In 1981

吾国吾民

老辈们的感情表达方式
堪称世界奇葩

暗送秋波时
说：杀千刀!

眼泪汪汪时
说：该死的!

泪流满面时
说：不要脸!

这么会这样
心口不一啊!

打是亲骂是爱
不打不骂是祸害!

这些不仅仅是
日常生活习惯

它折射出英雄时代的
刀光剑影

2011,8,5

My Country And My People

The way older people express their feelings
Is a wonderful flower in the world

As looking at each other in love
Say: you shoold be kill thousands of knives!

As full of tears in eyes
Say: Damn it!

With tears streaming down face
Say: Shame on you!

Why this will happen
What a difference!

Beating is kissing and scolding is love
Do not beat, do not scold is evil!

These are just
Daily living habits

And it reflects in the heroic age
Swords fighting

2011,8,5

生命的苹果

（一）

当早春清新的微风轻轻掠过缀花的草地和摇动的柳梢
和煦的阳光在湖面绿色透明的微波上轻快地跳跃
幼小的婴儿在母亲揪心的爱怜的目光的波涛中无忧无虑地飘摇
生机勃勃的小小的鲜亮的生命的光芒可爱地闪耀

在全世界的狂喜的滂沱的泪洪里、在幼小的朦胧的困乏中
有力地扭动着小小的令人无比疼爱的肢体
用那比全宇宙最美妙的歌声更为动人的嘹亮而高亢的呐喊
向全宇宙骄傲地宣告着一个崭新世界的辉煌的新生

在最博大无私的柔情和爱怜的泪洪中漂浮的
在充满无限慈爱的温柔的光芒的环护和照耀下
承载着我们对生活未来的最热切的期盼和梦想
不正是那高声地呼喊着可爱的生命的最美妙的乐章的生命的苹果吗？

（二）

当五月温暖的和风欢快地吹过那些白色豪华的亭台和回廊
眩目的阳光在锦簇的花团和少女们美丽的衣裙之间令人眼花缭乱地回照
深深的笑靥的小小的可爱的阴影里满藏着纯洁的热情和美丽的羞涩
透明的飞动的裙角和发梢在明媚的阳光中尽情地嬉戏、欢快地奔跑、跳跃和光艳夺目地闪耀

无忧无虑的、比世界上任何美妙的音乐更为美妙动人的银铃般清脆的笑声
是滋润人们充满爱怜的心田的生命的琼浆
那即将成熟的花蕾般的温柔的胸怀
在花团怒放的变幻的光影中可爱地轻轻地跳动

在我们最纯洁柔美的心灵深处
最优雅地拨动我们灵魂的竖琴的最美丽而敏感的可爱的冲动
使那最清纯而羞涩的少年人的痴心被最甜美而神秘的想象而迷恋和潦倒
不正是那最鲜活动人、最美妙神秘的生命的苹果吗?

（三）

当高耸的、开满硕大美丽的花朵的大树
在七月的热风中欢乐地喧哗、尽情地舞蹈
太阳的灼热的光焰
在姹紫嫣红的山谷中令人目眩地辉煌地返照

当爱的洪峰冲决了世间所有的堤防
在那些繁花怒放的喧哗的花树之间
晕头转向的美丽的小鸟的活泼的生命的双翼
被激情的风暴纷纷地吹乱

失去控制的无力的鸟儿在巨大的幸福的眩晕和恣意的尖叫、呻吟中
向着激情勃发的无底的深渊飞速地滑落
那不就是生命的苹果在爱的波涛中猛烈地颠动
在情热的激流中迷乱地旋转和沉浮?

（四）

在深秋和严冬的寒风凛冽的深夜
即使在那人生最悲恸、绝望的时刻
当我们仰望那繁星密布的宏伟庄严的浩瀚的星空
我们的思绪将会到达那由无数辉煌的世界的阵列组成的伟大宇宙的星辰之海的无限遥远的远方

但只要当我们想到在这浩瀚无际的宇宙之中
有那么一个无比可爱的充满光明和温暖的伟大的家园
用她无比醇美甘甜的乳汁哺育着我们有着无比精美神奇功能的身体和充满美丽激情的高贵的心灵
在我们心灵的天空中就会立刻充满着无比浩大的光明与温暖的洪流
我们的心中就会升起一种无与伦比的巨大的骄傲和幸福
在泪雨滂沱中满怀着对伟大的造物力量的无比的感激之情

不论我们的思绪或者身体可能到达那浩瀚宇宙的多么遥远的远方
但在我们心灵世界的最庄严肃穆的殿堂，在我们最悠远深沉的梦幻之乡
那个在伟大的太阳的永恒的五彩斑斓的辉煌而温暖的慈光的环护和照耀之中
庄严地缓慢地旋转着，并闪烁着神奇而无比美丽的蔚蓝色的光芒
不就是我们灵魂深处那无比可爱的、永恒的、伟大而慈祥的生命的苹果吗？

2002.1.22

Apple Of Life

(I)

When fresh breeze of early spring sweeps gently over flowery meadows and swaying willows
The warm sun danced lightly on transparent green waves of the lake
The little baby was floating carefree in waves of her mother's heart-wrenching loving eyes
The light of the little living of bright life shone lovingly

In the rushing tears of the world's ecstasy, in the misty drowsiness of young children
With a powerful twist of tiny, and incredibly loving limbs
With a shout louder and louder than the most beautiful song in all the universe
It is proudly proclaiming to the whole universe the glorious birth of a new world

Floating in the flood of tears of the greatest unselfish tenderness and love
Surrounded and illuminated by a gentle light filled with infinite love
It carries our most ardent hopes and dreams for the future of life
Is it not the apple of life that cries out the most beautiful music of lovely life?

(2)

When May warm breeze blows merrily through white and luxurious pavilions and cloisters
Sun shines dazzlingly back and forth between colorful clusters of flowers and girls' nice dresses

The little lovely shadows of a deep smile are full of pure passion and beautiful shyness
Transparent flying skirts and hair tips play in bright sunshine, running,jumping,shining brightly

A carefree, silvery sound of laughter is more beautiful than any music in the world
It is the milk of life that moistens people's hearts full of love and compassion
That is about to mature bud like tender mind
Dancing gently in the changing light and shadow of the flowers in full bloom

In the most pure and soft of our hearts. The most beautiful and sensitive lovely impulses the most gracefully harp plucking our soul. So that the purest and shy young man infatuated with the most sweet and mysterious imagination and down.
Is not it the apple of the most vivid, beautiful and mysterious life?

(3)

When the tall trees, full of big and beautiful flowers
In the hot air of July, the noise of joy, dance to the heart's content
The scorching flame of the sun reflects
A dazzling light in a valley of brilliant colors

When the flood of love breaks all the embankments of the world
Among the noisy trees in full bloom
Giddy beautiful bird on the wings of lively life
Was blown apart by the storms of passion

The powerless bird out of control in a big dizzy happiness and a wanton shriek and groan
Hurtling down the bottomless abyss of passion
It is not the apple of life violently tossed in the waves of love

Whirling and sinking in the rapids of emotional heat?

(4)

In the cold, cold night of late autumn and winter
Even in the darkest, most hopeless moments of life
When we look up at the starry, majestic vastness of the sky. Our thoughts will reach the infinite distance of the sea, stars, great universe made up of countless splendid arrays of worlds

But when we think about the immensity of the universe
There is such a lovely great home full of light and warmth
With her very mellow and sweet milk, we have a very exquisite and magical function of the body and a noble soul full of beautiful passion. The sky of our heart is immediately filled with a vast flood of light and warmth. There will arise in our hearts a great pride and happiness that cannot be matched. In the rain of tears was filled with great gratitude to the great force of creation.

No matter how far our mind or body may reach into that vast expanse of space
But in the most solemn hall of our spiritual world, in our deepest and deepest dreamland
The one that is surrounded and illuminated by the eternal, colorful splendor and warm mercy of the great sun. It whirls majestically and slowly, and glows with a magical and wonderfully beautiful azure light. Is it not the apple of the inestimably lovely, eternal, great and kind life in the depths of our souls?

2002.1.22

大 刀

大刀向鬼子头上砍去
但是在这之前
大刀也曾经
向锐意变革的人们头上砍去

大刀向鬼子头上砍去
可是凶恶的侵略者的
暴雨般的炮弹
也向国人的头上落下去

大刀固然英勇
可歌可泣
但是终敌不过
侵略者的大炮

假若我们的大刀
不是曾经忙于屠杀有志于变革的人们
也许后来就不必用我们的血肉之躯
与敌人的大炮相拼

2015.1.13

A Big Knife

A big knife chopped to the devil's head
But before that
The big knife once
Chopped to the people who wanted to change their minds

A big knife chopped to the devil's head
But the rain-like artillery shells
Of the vicious invaders
Also fell on the head of the Chinese people

The big knife, heroic
Can be sung and shed tears
But can not stop the cannon
Of invaders

If our big knife
Have not been busy slaughtering those people who have the idea to change their minds
Maybe there was no need to use our flesh and blood
To fight with the enemy's cannon

2015.1.3

假 如

假如甲午不败
现在的中国
仍然还是腐朽的封建王朝
怎能有中国的新生

假如甲午不败
现在的中国人
可能仍然是
百年前的德性

太监横行
嫔妃成群
当官的头插野鸡毛
长袍马褂马蹄袖

天朝的臣民们
五体投地
诚惶诚恐
万岁，万岁，万万岁！渣！

2014.7.3

If

If the Sino Japanese War in 1895 was undefeated
In China now
It is still the decaying feudal dynasty
How can there be a new life in China

If the Sino Japanese War in 1895 was undefeated
Chinese now
May still be virtue
As a hundred years ago

Eunuchs run amok
Consorts of concubines
Heads of leaders inserted pheasant feathers
In long gown, Mandarin coat, horse hooves and sleeves

People of China
Throwing their body on the ground
Sincerely
Long live, long live, long live! Zhe!

2014.7.3

● **World Poetry Comments**

CHENG YIN – A master of metaphysical Yang and Yin

By Lanka Siva Rama Prasad [India]
English to Chinese Translated by Sophy Chen [China]

I

Once upon a time there was a war between the tree kingdoms of Philosophy and poetry. Socrates, Aristotle, Plotinus, Augustine, Boethius, Aquinas, Hegel were the warrior philosopher branches whereas Kant, Kierkegaard, Dilthey, Nietzsche, Heidegger, Ferdinand de Saussure, Paul de Man, Jacques Derrida were the poetry soldier branches. And many visionaries joined this or that side and the quarrel never stopped and is evident even today.

Then the tree of philosophy grew into a big one and it has as many fruitful branches as many of its followers and poetree or poetry tree too grew but it has not so many branches but more leaves, flowers and fruits.

The Chinese trees of Philosophy and poetry have their roots in antiquity the main branches and bonsai varieties bore the inscriptions of Shang Di, Tian- Heaven, Ming- destiny, de- virtue; Dao- the Way; ren- Humanity, love; yi- righteousness; and yin-yang elements of cosmic order or disorder;

Kong Fuzi (Confucius) (551–479 BCE) -a wandering philosopher proposed Dao is the way of ancient kings, the way of virtue and the way of man; whereas to Laozi Dao is the way of Nature; the Buddhist influence brought the thoughts about the Ultimate Reality as being or non-being; Human nature as li; and qi- the universal essence; and the Marxist influence and the influence of western philosophers brought new branches with many metallic hues to both philosophical and poetry trees.

Five constant virtues – benevolence- ren; righteousness- vi; wisdom- zhi; trustworthiness- xin; propriety- li; and the ethical obligations of children to their parents or care for others- filial piety or filiality have become obligations of day to day life and those thoughts were mirrored in Chinese philosophy and poetry.

One day Zi Gong [a disciple] asked his master Kong Fuzi: "Is there any one word that could guide a person throughout life?"

The Master replied: "How about 'reciprocity'! Never impose on others what you would not choose for yourself."

This has become a golden rule in the everyday life of Chinese people and their vision.

The Master said, "My children, why do you not study the Book of Poetry?

"The Odes serve to stimulate the mind.

"They may be used for purposes of self-contemplation.

"They teach the art of sociability.

"They show how to regulate feelings of resentment.

"From them you learn the more immediate duty of serving one's father, and the remoter one of serving one's country.

"From them we become largely acquainted with the names of birds, beasts, and plants.

Then someone said:

What's in a name? That which we call a Rose
By any other name would smell as sweet-

-Romeo- Juliet Act 2- Scene 2- William Shakespeare

Then the Master said, "that it may be true with flowers and lovers, but
If names be not correct, language is not in accordance with the truth of things.

If language be not in accordance with the truth of things, affairs cannot be carried on to success.

When affairs cannot be carried on to success, proprieties and music do not flourish.

When proprieties and music do not flourish, punishments will not be properly awarded.

When punishments are not properly awarded, the people do not know how to move hand or foot.

Therefore a superior man considers it necessary that the names he uses may be spoken appropriately, and also that what he speaks may be carried out appropriately. What the superior man requires is just that in his words there may be nothing incorrect."

(- Xun Zi- chapter (22) "On the Rectification of Names" claims the ancient sage-kings chose names)

It is so as we go up and up we can see the world scene more and more-

bái rì yī shān jìn,
huáng hé rù hǎi liú;
yù qióng qiān lǐ mù,
gèng shàng yì céng lóu.

The sun sets behind the mountains,
and the Yellow River flows into the sea.
To thoroughly enjoy a thousand-mile sight,
climb up another level

— 王之涣 (Wang Zhihuan)

That reminds me a poem by Li Bai- 701–762), also pronounced as (Li Bo or Taibai was a Chinese poet, acclaimed from his own time to the present as a brilliant and romantic figure who took traditional poetic forms to new heights. under the Tang dynasty which is often called the Golden Age of poetry". The expression "Three Wonders" denotes Pei Min's swordplay, Zhang Xu's calligraphy and Li Bai's poetry.

The living one is a passing traveller
The dead, a man come home.
One brief journey between Heaven and Earth
Then alas! We are the same old dust of ten thousand age

- Li Bai

II.

Qingdao Chen Yin, ID name: Zhang Ronggui, net name: Chen Yin, born in 1949, a retired mechanical engineer, lives in Qindao. He began to write modern poems at the age of 20, began to publish his modern poems on the Internet in 2011 and has published a collection of poetry titled “Dust Poetry Collection” in 2017.

A visionary and mystic poet Chen Yin ponders into the metaphysical and mundane worlds, finds the wonders of universe in their pristine form and paints them with vivid colours of his palette. His poems are the statements of human impressions in imaginative terms connecting thing up above and low below. He expresses the high-flown truth of signs on life’s great instances.

Pulvis et umbra sumus- we are but dust and shadow -says Horace on his odes... likewise Chen Yin wonders-

Above these flickering
And floating dust
If there are also countless
Tiny, and lovely lives living

Above them and there how many dramas
Of their own lives have been played
How many hopes and disappointments
Joy and sorrow are there?

Our soul is often full of humble and material desires, there is no ideal starlight in the dark night sky of our soul, even if there is an occasional inspiration lightning cutting through the dark clouds, when the clumsy pen tip records it in a hurry, the words on the paper have lost its original precious spiritual light. The poet says the Creator is like an artist blowing golden spirit to candy, and when he looks at us, is he filled with full of pride or full of disappointment? And when the curtain has fallen down on the stage, we look like tiny dust particles. The Ages of sand sifts over human impermanence, untrod and traceless, unremembering and unvital.

The high tower on the beach
Majestically standing
Is a great work built carefully
By an ambitious boy

However, whenever he is about to complete
His unprecedented great cause
The waves have always gently swept down the tower
laughing mischievously

Why? His question reverberates in its entirety in the entirety. The poet finds the Creator as a puppeteer with strings in his hand manipulating the people made from the dust. In a moment of privilege doused with epiphany, vision and choice, poet Chen Yin reverts back to nature. He finds the metaphorical swan, hawk, moth, fire, peach pits, golden rainbow dreams, pains, meditation, and man's unquenchable thirst to find better things often ending in disappointment, total recalls, reincarnation, and the duality of happiness and pain, his pen becomes word bearer sword-

If in front of the sunny window
In intoxicating blowing of the spring breeze
I held a shinning pen
There are thousands of sirens calling angrily in my heart

...

When my excited pen
Breaks the calm of the manuscript paper
There will be the voice of steel rolling and ringing
And the bombardment voice of light and thunder

He sees evil and good in their raw state, evil in winning spree, life moving painfully slow, and man hardly knows how to play it.

What the greatest pain to a man
Is that nothing is worth to die for
And he does not know what to do on with life

It was too long to be fooled by the mirage
Once he sees clearly everything that makes him excited
His mind will be overwhelmed by the deserted sand

Poet Chen Yin with his conceits or extended metaphors like John Donne, Henry Vaughan, Andrew Marvel and George Hubert brought his poetry to a new level. His poetic statements are imbued with wisdom and subtlety.

In the presence of God
There is no honorable and humble
In the face of true feelings
There is no beauty and ugly

But no matter where I am in the world
My heart always stays beside my mother
My hometown and mother that I've been away for a long time, oh
Do you know the melancholy of a traveler?

Here I have mentioned a few lines of our mystic and nature poet Chen Yin. His poems are profound in nature and dignified in their rendering and quintessential in their framing. His poems are brief in their length but deep in their aesthetic values.

In the east of the mountains (Shandong), in the cyan city Qingdao, Cheng Yin successfully yields a great pen with fine nib and paints and writes the poems that links the Heaven and Earth.

III

chú hé rì dāng wǔ,
hàn dī hé xià tǔ.
shuí zhī pán zhōng cān,
lì lì jiē xīn kǔ.

Cultivating grains at noon,
Sweat dripping into the earth beneath.
Who would have thought the food on your plate,

each and every grain, came from hard work?

- 李绅 (Li Shen)

Sophy Chen is a world acclaimed poet and translator, hard working in nature, serene and beautiful in appearance took a gigantic task of bringing Chinese modern poetry in to the English-speaking world. Her relentless efforts brought poets together and built timeless bridges between neighboring cultures. She has been doing it with such grit and passion it makes the observers awestruck.

She has translated her fellow poets' poems into English with such dexterity and style they look original and lively.

A Big Knife

A big knife chopped the devil's head
But before that
The big knife once
Chopped the people who wanted to change their minds

A big knife that chopped the devil's head, but the rain-like artillery shells, Of the vicious invaders also fell on the head of the Chinese people; The big knife, heroic can be sung and shed tears but cannot stop the cannon of the invaders

If our big knife has not been busy
slaughtering those people who have the idea to change their minds
Maybe there was no need to use our flesh and blood
To fight the enemy's cannon-

This multi-layered poem aptly describes the worthiness of the poet Cheng Yin and the translator Sophy Chen. I wish them all the success and fame they deserve.

"For if we're destroyed, the knowledge is dead...We're nothing more than dust jackets for books...so many pages to a person..."

— Ray Bradbury, Fahrenheit 451

尘音——玄学阴阳大师

作者：[印度]兰卡·斯瓦·罗摩·普拉萨德
译者：[中国]苏菲(英译汉)

一

从前，三个王国在哲学和诗歌之间发生了一场战争。苏格拉底、亚里士多德、普罗提诺、奥古斯丁、波伊提乌、阿奎那、黑格尔是哲学家战士的分支，而康德、克尔凯郭尔、狄尔泰、尼采、海德格尔、费迪南德·德索绪尔、保罗·德曼、雅克·德里达是诗歌战士的分支。许多有远见的人加入了这一方或那一方，争吵从未停止，即使在今天也很明显。

然后，哲学之树长成了一棵大树，它的枝叶和它的追随者一样多，而诗歌之树也长大了，但它没有那么多的枝叶，却有更多的叶子、花朵和果实。

中国的哲学树和诗歌树源远流长，主要的枝干和盆景品种上都有"上-上帝"、"天-上天"、"命-命运"、"德-道德"、道-道路、人-人性、爱、义-公义、阴-阳元素的宇宙秩序或无序；

孔夫子(孔子)(公元前551-479年)是一位流浪哲学家，他提出道是古代君王之道、德性之道、人性之道；而老子的道则是自然之道；佛教的影响带来了终极实相的存在或非存在的思想；人性如利；气-宇宙的本质；马克思主义和西方哲学家的影响为哲学和诗歌之树带来了许多金属色彩的新分支。

三纲五常——仁义礼智信。子女对父母或照顾他人的道德义务——孝顺或不孝顺已经成为日常生活的义务，这些思想反映在中国的哲学和诗歌中。

一天，子贡问他的师父孔夫子 :“ 有没有一句话可以指导一个人的一生 ?”

孔子回答说 :“‘ 互惠 ’ 呢 ? 己所不欲，勿施于人。”

这已经成为中国人日常生活和视野中的黄金法则。

孔子说 :“ 孩子们，你们为什么不学习《诗经》呢 ?

“ 颂歌是用来刺激心灵的。

它们可能用于自我沉思。

“ 他们教授社交的艺术。

“ 它们展示了如何调节怨恨情绪。

“ 从他们那里，你学到更直接的责任是为父亲服务，以及更长远的责任是为国家服务。

从他们那里，我们大致熟悉了鸟类、野兽和植物的名字。

然后有人说 :

名字里有什么 ? 我们称之为玫瑰的东西

任何别的名字闻起来都一样甜美

——《罗密欧与朱丽叶》第二幕 - 第二场 —— 威廉 · 莎士比亚

孔子说 :“ 花和恋人也许是这样，但是

如果名称不正确，语言就不符合事物的真相。

如果语言不符合事物的真相，事情就不能取得成功。

当事情不能顺利进行时，礼仪和音乐就不会蓬勃发展。

当礼乐不兴盛时，惩罚就不会得到适当的奖励。

当惩罚没有得到适当的奖励时，人们不知道如何移动手脚。

因此，一个优秀的人认为，他所使用的名字必须恰当地说出，他所说的话也必须恰当地执行。君子所要求的只是他的话中不能有任何错误。”

(—— 荀子 —— 第二十二章)《正名论》声称古代圣贤王选名)

是这样，当我们越爬越高，我们看到的景色世界就越来越多 :

白日依山尽，黄河入海流。
欲穷千里目，更上一层楼。

太阳快落山了，

黄河流入大海。
纵览千里风光，
爬上另一层楼。
—— 王之涣

这让我想起了李白 (701-762) 的一首诗，也读作李波或太白，是一位中国诗人，从他自己的时代到现在，都被誉为是一个才华横溢、浪漫的人物，他把传统的诗歌形式推向了新的高度。唐朝被称为诗歌的黄金时代。“ 三绝 ” 指的是裴旻的剑术、张旭的书法和李白的诗歌。

活着的人是一个过客；
人死了，一个人回家了。
一次短暂的天地之旅
然后唉！我们都是一样的万年尘埃
—— 李白

二

青岛尘音，真名：张荣贵，网名：尘音，1949 年生，退休机械工程师，现居青岛。20 岁开始写现代诗，2011 年开始在网上发表现代诗，2017 年出版诗集《尘诗集》。

诗人尘音是一位富有远见和神秘精神的诗人，他对玄学世界和世俗世界进行了深入的思考，发现了宇宙中最原始的奇迹，并用他的调色板上生动的色彩描绘了这些奇迹。他的诗是对人类印象的陈述，并用富有想象力的方式将上下事物联系起来。他在生命的伟大实例中表达了崇高的真理。

“Pulvis et umbra sumus”—— 我们不过是尘埃和影子 —— 贺拉斯在他的颂歌中如是说。同样，尘音也想知道

在这些闪烁的
浮动的尘埃上面
是否也生活着无数的
微小的可爱的生命

在那上面也曾上演过多少
他们自己的生活的戏剧
也曾有多少希望与失望
欢乐与悲伤？

我们的灵魂往往充满了卑微和物质的欲望，在我们灵魂黑暗的夜空中没有理想的星光，即使偶尔有灵感的闪电划过乌云，当笨拙的笔尖匆忙记录下来时，纸上的文字也失去了原来珍贵的精神之光。诗人说造物主就像一个艺术家把金色的精灵吹到糖果上，当他看着我们的时候，他是充满了骄傲还是充满了失望？当舞台上的帷幕落下时，我们看起来就像微小的尘埃颗粒。沙尘的年代筛过人类的无常，未被践踏而无迹可寻，被遗忘而无生气。

沙滩上的高塔
雄伟地耸立着
是雄心勃勃的男孩
精心建造的伟大作品

可是，每当他即将完成
空前伟大的事业
海浪总要恶作剧地嘻笑着
将高塔轻轻冲倒

为什么？他的问题引起了广泛的反响。诗人发现造物主就像一个操纵木偶的人，手里拿着线，操纵着尘土所造的人。在顿悟、远见和选择的特权时刻，诗人尘音回归自然。他找到了天鹅、鹰、蛾、火、桃核、金色彩虹的梦想、痛苦、沉思，以及人类对更好事物的不可抑制的渴望，这些渴望往往总以失望、回忆、轮回、快乐与痛苦的二元性而告终，他的笔变成了手里的剑。

若在那阳光灿烂的窗前
在春风醉人的吹拂之中
我提起了闪光的钢笔
心中有万千支号角怒鸣

……

当我的激动的笔锋
搅扰了稿纸的平静
那里将滚动着钢铁的铿锵
和雷电的轰隆

他看到恶与善的原始状态，看到恶在胜利的狂欢中，看到生命缓慢得令人痛苦，而人类几乎不知道如何去玩。

人最大的痛苦
是没有什么值得去死
而活着又不知为了什么

被海市蜃楼愚弄得太久
一旦看清使他激动的一切
心田也将被荒沙淹没

诗人尘音像约翰·多恩、亨利·沃恩、安德鲁·马维尔和乔治·休伯特一样，用他的自傲或延伸的隐喻把他的诗歌提升到一个新的水平。他的诗句充满智慧和微妙。

在上帝的面前
没有什么尊卑
在真情的面前
没有什么美丑

可是，不管我在世界上什么地方
我的心总是留在母亲身旁
我久违的故乡、母亲哟
你可知道游子的惆怅？

在这里我提到了我们神秘的，自然主义诗人尘音的几句诗。他的诗，质地深刻，手法庄重，结构精辟。他的诗，虽短小精悍，但具有深厚的审美价值。

在山之东（山东），青色之城青岛，尘音成功地拿出一支笔尖细腻的大笔，写出了连接天地的诗篇。

三

锄禾日当午，汗滴禾下土。
谁知盘中餐，粒粒皆辛苦？

中午种谷粒，
汗水滴落在脚下的泥土里。
谁能想到你盘子里的食物，
每一粒粮食，都来自辛勤劳动呢？
——李申

苏菲是一位享誉世界的诗人和翻译家，她天生勤奋，外表宁静美丽，肩负着将中国现代诗歌引入英语世界的艰巨任务。她不懈的努力使诗人们走到一起，在邻近的文化之间架起了永恒的桥梁。她一直在以如此的勇气和激情做这件事，让旁观者肃然起敬。

她把其他诗人的诗翻译成英文，既灵巧又有风格，看起来新颖而生动：

大刀

大刀向鬼子头上砍去
但是在这之前
大刀也曾经
向锐意变革的人们头上砍去

大刀向鬼子头上砍去
可是凶恶的侵略者的
暴雨般的炮弹
也向国人的头上落下去

大刀固然英勇
可歌可泣
但是终敌不过

侵略者的大炮

假若我们的大刀
不是曾经忙于屠杀有志于变革的人们
也许后来就不必用我们的血肉之躯
与敌人的大炮相拼

这首多层次的诗恰如其分地描述了诗人尘音和翻译家苏菲绮丽的价值。我希望他们获得应得的成功和声誉。

“因为如果我们被毁灭了，知识也就死了 …… 我们只不过是书的防尘套 …… 一个人要写那么多页 ……”

——雷 · 布拉德伯里 , 华氏 451 度

※※※※※※※※※※※※※※※※※※※※※※※※※※※

[India] Lanka Siva Rama Prasad
[印度] 兰卡 · 斯瓦 · 罗摩 · 普拉萨德

Renowned author, distinguished cartoonist, painter, critic, editor and speaker. Host and sponsor of Pentasi B India World Poetry Festival. Winner of the Sophy Chen World Poetry Prize.

兰卡 · 斯瓦 · 罗摩 · 普拉萨德，著名作家、杰出漫画家、画家、评论家、编辑和演说家。Pentasi B 印度世界诗歌节主办人和赞助商。苏菲世界诗歌奖获奖者。

作者后记

在大约十七、八岁时，那时还是文革当中，从朋友那里借到一本"裴多菲诗选"，那是我第一次接触"新诗"。从那以后，就开始了与新诗结缘。

在那无比荒谬的，所谓"无比优越"的动乱年代，在那些有职业的人们都疯狂地互相狂吠撕咬时，我们社会青年是没有资格参加那场所谓伟大的运动的。我们是一群被社会抛弃的，不在册的，最低贱的人。那时的所谓真理是有文化就是反动、有罪，我们因为认几个字就成为需要接受"再教育"的罪人，等待我们的命运只能是"上山下乡"，被发配，充军，而且只能在那里扎根，开花，结果，永远不许回城，自生自灭，无人过问。我们心中的痛苦，绝望与悲愤可想而知。就不由自主地将这些情绪诉诸笔端。因而产生了像'钢笔'这类的极端叛逆的作品，这些作品显然受到裴多菲的影响。艺术形式上肯定幼稚而粗糙。

就这样断断续续地学习写作，从未有发表的想法。直到2011年，在学习电脑时偶然发现了网络诗坛这一新生事物，之后就开始在半岛诗坛上发表作品。

我天生笨拙，年轻时也曾试图学习现代的、陌生化的或者荒诞的写作技法，但是始终学不会也写不出那种莫测高深的诗篇。当时感到很失落，但现在想来则有点庆幸。

我写的作品都很浅显易懂，只要识字的平凡的人们都能读懂，希望他们能喜欢，并愿与他们共同思考自然与人生。

我虽然学的是中文，也喜欢读唐诗宋词，但不喜欢用文言写作，因为现在的人们大多读不懂文言，我们应该为现在的人们写作。

去年秋天，在半岛诗坛荷东版主老师的热情鼓励支持下，我决定将此前不多的作品结集出版。借此机会，向多年来对我悉心指导与鼓励的荷东版主老师和诸位版主老师和诸位网友老师表示衷心感谢。衷心感谢荷东版主老师在百忙之中抽时间为小册子写了读后感。但老师在读后感中说了过多的溢美之辞，使我十分惶恐不安。

青岛尘音（张荣桂）
2017.3　青岛家中

Afterword Of Author

When I was about 17 or 18 years old, in the midst of the Cultural Revolution, I borrowed from a friend, a copy of the Selected Poems of Pablo Neruda, which was my first contact with "new poetry". From then on, I began to get attached to new poetry.

The youth of our society were not qualified to take part in that great movement in those absurd, "superior" times of turmoil, when all those who had careers were barking and biting each other madly. We are a group of social outcasts, unregistered, the lowest of the low class. The so-called truth at that time was that culture was reactionary and sinful, that we became sinners who needed to be "re-educated" because we confessed a few words, and that our fate could only be "going up the mountain to the countryside", being sent and deported, and that we could only take root there, blossom and bear fruit, and never be allowed to return to the city, fend for ourselves, and no one asked. You can imagine the pain, the despair, the anger in our hearts. I can't help but write about these feelings. This resulted in extremely rebellious works such as the "Pen", which was clearly influenced by Pablo Neruda. The art form must be childish and crude.

So I learned to write on and off, and never had the idea of publishing. It was not until 2011, when i was studying computer, that i accidentally discovered the Internet poetry world and began to publish my works on the Peninsula Poetry Circle.

I was clumsy by nature, and when I was young I tried to learn modern, strange, or absurd writing techniques, but I could not learn and could not write such a profound poem. I was disappointed, but now I think I'm glad.

Although I studied Chinese and like to read Tang and Song poems, I don't like to write in classical Chinese, because most people today can't read classical Chinese, and we should write for people today.

Last autumn, with the warm encouragement and support of He Dong, the moderator of the Peninsula Poetry Circle, I decided to collect and publish my few works. I would like to take this opportunity to express my heartfelt thanks to moderator He Dong and teachers who have carefully guided and encouraged me over the years. I sincerely thank the moderator and teacher He Dong for taking time out of his busy schedule to write the reading comments for the booklet. However, the teacher said too much praise in the reading, which made me very nervous.

Qingdao Cheng Yin (Zhang Ronggui)
2017.3 at home in Qingdao

Qingdao Cheng Yin's Chinese Poetry Collection Translated by Sophy Chen
苏菲英译青岛尘音汉语诗歌集

尘埃集
Dust Poetry Collection

作者：青岛尘音
Author: Qingdao Cheng Yin

Translator：Sophy Chen / Lihua Chen
译 者：苏 菲 / 陈丽华
Chief Editor：Sophy Chen / Lihua Chen
主 编：苏 菲 / 陈丽华

Publisher：Sophy International Translation Publishing House
出版社：苏菲国际翻译出版社
ISBN / 书号：ISBN 978-988-79632-5-7

Edited And Published："Sophy Poetry & Translation" C-E World Poetry Paper Magazine
编辑出版：《苏菲诗歌 & 翻译》英汉纸质世界诗刊社
Editor：Dazang Chen, Sophy Chen
编 辑：大 藏、苏 菲
Cover Design：Sophy Chen, Dazang Chen
封面设计：苏 菲、大 藏
Layout Design：Dazang Chen
排 版：大 藏

Address：Room 1609, Kowloon Bank, 555, Littleton Road, Mongkok, Kowloon, Hong Kong
通讯地址：香港九龙旺角弥顿道 555 号九龙行 1609 室
Country：[China] HKSAR
国 家：[中国] 香港特区
Folio：5.5x8.5 inch
开 本：5.5x8.5 英寸
Amount：0001-2000 copies
印 数：0001-2000 册
Edition：First print on October 25 2023
版 次：2023 年 10 月 25 日第 1 次印刷
Price：CNY 300 HKD 620 USD 140
定 价：人民币 300 元 港币 620 元 美元 140 元

Tel / 微信 & 电话 : 18201007874
https://www.sophypoetry.com

www.ingramcontent.com/pod-product-compliance
Lightning Source LLC
LaVergne TN
LVHW010553160826
845677LV00013B/3117